The Making *of*
a Martyr

Father Richard Novak, C.S.C.

The Making *of* *a* Martyr

Father Richard Novak, C.S.C.

Mary Ann Novak

Published in the United States of America
by The Novak Family Foundation, Inc.
www.thenovakfoundation.org

The Making of a Martyr: Father Richard Novak, C.S.C.
Novak, Mary Ann

Cover Art Copyright © Karen Laub-Novak
Cover Design by Jonathan Hartland

ISBN: 1-4944396-6-2
ISBN-13: 978-1-4944396-6-8

*Dedicated to Michael J. and Irene L. Novak,
who gave their son freely to serve God
on Earth and in Heaven.*

Contents

Preface   9

Introduction by Michael Novak   15

I. Early Life, Notre Dame, and   19
    Novitiate

II. Studying at Stonehill and in France   29

III. Life as a Missionary in East Pakistan   47

IV. Death in East Pakistan   57

V. Remembrances and Reminders   73

VI. Conclusion   83

Afterword   89

Appendix: Funeral Eulogy   93

About the Author   103

Preface

The day I learned that Richard had disappeared was a normal school day for me, a freshman in high school and the only one of the five children still at home. As I did the dishes that Monday evening of January 20th, 1964, I was preoccupied with a situation at school and not listening to my father on the phone behind me, nor inquiring into why my Mother was crying into the dish towel. But when my father hung up the phone, I heard a large sigh from him, normally a signal of a serious situation, and I spun around saying: what's the matter? My father sighed loudly again and told me my brother was missing, not Michael as we already feared since he was two days late in returning from Rome, but Richard in East Pakistan. Richard missing, I thought? He was already missing on the other side of the world to this 15 year old teenager, and the days that followed were as mysterious as that news. Admonished by my parents to keep the news to myself, the first thing I did later that night was to secretly call my next oldest brother Ben to come home immediately from Penn State.

An article on Richard's disappearance speculating in ghoulish detail on what might have happened to him greeted us all the next morning, and although my father insisted I go to school that day, he didn't insist after that. Nor did my parents question why Ben was home. They retreated to their bedroom for several days, leaving Ben and I to deal with the constant ringing of the doorbell and the telephone. Not only did every person in our predominantly Jewish neighborhood decamp to our home, but I answered calls from friends, relatives, the press, and even spoke directly to President Lyndon B. Johnson who called without benefit of a secretary as intermediary. But none of these brought news that Richard was found.

The events that followed in the subsequent weeks are both clear as carved glass in my mind and blurred by the rapidity of a funeral without a body within a week of being told of his disappearance. The total lack of knowledge of what happened to Richard, our sweetest brother, gave it all a veneer of unreality. The Family either didn't tell me as the youngest what was going on or they just came to accept that we didn't know the answer, and weren't going to get many details or clear answers, so there was nothing to discuss. Our lives moved on with only the undercurrent of Richard being absent, truly

MIA as we say now, and a sense that somehow he or we were at fault for his disappearance. Sometimes, it seems that the victim is the one person overlooked, ignored, forgotten: a cluster of translucent, conflicting memories refracted through other people's words.

In 2003 I received an email from Joseph, the son of my deceased brother Jim, about the death of a prominent and well-respected journalist friend of his, Manu Kabir, whom I had met several times. Manu had been imprisoned for political reasons in Dacca, East Pakistan, in the late 1960s before fierce war of independence was won from Pakistan in 1971. During Manu's time in prison, the email noted, the journalist's "bat boy," a convict-servant, was one of the murderers of Father Richard Novak, C.S.C., a popular professor at the respected Notre Dame College in Dhaka (formerly Dacca, spelling changed in 1983), now the capital of the newly independent country of Bangladesh. Who this convict-servant was exactly, what his name was, what he did and why, remain mysteries in a long line of them. We believe that he was likely released in the general amnesty granted prisoners by the new Bangladeshi government in 1972.

Having been a young teenager of 13 when Father Richard left to be a missionary, this sudden reference caught my attention. I had thought of Richard less and less over time, for his mysterious and confusing disappearance had resulted in his memory fading, almost as if he had never been real. The living Richard was erased by his shocking but undefined death, and this suppression allowed me to ignore any urgent fireworks left behind. Now I became determined to find out what happened, to in effect 'resurrect' Richard, the sweetest of brothers.

This set me to pondering that time in my memory, questioning our eldest brother Michael on what he knew, and on beginning a slow effort to find family files and records on Richard, even while working more than full time. As I became more immersed in relearning about Richard's life and death, the recommendation that I consider presenting a paper to the Holy Cross History Association became a goad to getting down in writing his story as thoroughly as I could. This short book of research thus was originally prepared for the 2008 Holy Cross History Conference in Salt Lake City as an exploration of the life and death of my brother.

I am deeply grateful to the Holy Cross Priests, Brothers and employees who so warmly welcomed and assisted me. They had not forgotten Richard and were glad we were seeking to bring his story forward. The available resources available were tremendous, including the Holy Cross Eastern Province Archives in North Easton, MA; the Michael

Novak Archives at Stonehill College in North Easton, MA; the Foreign Mission Generalate in the archives of Notre Dame University, Notre Dame, IN; and the Holy Cross Indiana Province Archives at Notre Dame, IN.

The following are owed special acknowledgment for their invaluable support during the course of research: Fr. David Schlaver, C.S.C., Holy Cross Mission Archives, Notre Dame, Indiana; Fr. Richard W. Timm, C.S.C., Province Archives, Dhaka, Bangladesh; Fr. David Arthur, C.S.C., Province Archives, North Easton, Massachusetts; Nicole Tourangeau, Archivist, Papers of Michael Novak, Stonehill College, North Easton, Massachusetts; Fr. Chris Kuhn, C.S.C., Province Archives, Notre Dame, Indiana; Wm. Kevin Cawley, Archivist, University of Notre Dame, Notre Dame, Indiana, Bob Hannon, Office of Development, U.S. Province of Holy Cross, North Easton, Massachusetts. There are too many others to list by name.

I found the material providing much of the detail of what is known and understood about Father Novak's death, as well as heard the interpretive memories of many of Father Novak's friends and colleagues who answered my call. The outpouring of affection was deeply moving and exciting, as Richard came alive again for me. But reading the Journals and files of the search for him, as you will see in small part I provide here, was heartbreaking.

To those who knew Richard, he was lovable. I believe those just meeting him now, as the 50th anniversary of this young priest's death nears on January 16, 2014, will be glad they did.

Mary Ann Novak
Washington, DC

Introduction

This short book of research into the facts surrounding the death of our brother Richard J. Novak, a priest of Holy Cross slain on a mission of mercy, is amazingly timely. Richard's murder came at the tail-end of horrific Muslim-Hindu violence in East Pakistan (now Bangladesh) on January 16, 1964, whose 50th anniversary we now mark.

Mary Ann spent two years of intense effort in searching out records and archives as widely dispersed as Bangladesh and Massachusetts, interviewing those with first-hand knowledge of the very day of the murder and its long aftermath, writing letters to others whose names she came upon, comparing notes with other historians and archivists, and running down leads wherever they kept turning up. This was important because we had very few details on Richard's death. All this sometimes very taxing toil have borne magnificent fruit in this short book.

During the days after Father Richard's brutal death, very little was known to our family. We were told that he had disappeared amid the awful rioting of the time, during which thousands of slain bodies were thrown into the rivers. A little more than a week later, my father was told that it was a virtual certainty that our brother Dick was dead, and that it would be wise (especially for our mother) to go ahead with a funeral Mass, even though his body had not yet been found. In fact, as far as the family was ever told, the body was never found, although some personal items of his were eventually recovered—broken glasses, the bronze Holy Cross of the habit of the Congregation that he wore around his neck as he was slain, and a few other objects. Some years later his simple but beautifully wrought chalice (he had had it made in France, where he had been ordained) was brought back to the U.S. by Fr. Joseph Lehane, C.S.C. All these relics we sent to Stonehill College, his alma mater, in North Easton, Massachusetts, along with many of his papers.

There are still some mysteries (in a detective's sense) surrounding Father Richard's death, some unknowns. But Mary Ann's scrupulous research went a long way toward clearing up many of them, making some disappear, and bringing others into sharper relief.

As Father Richard's younger sister (and the youngest of the five of us), Mary Ann had a special experience of her older brother (thirteen years older, to be exact). The two of them were most affectionate toward one another, and the most connected. So the reader will almost certainly find that Mary Ann has made her dearest brother quite present in this short book of research, as he is present still to those who remember him.

Michael Novak
Lewes, Delaware

I.

Early Life, Notre Dame, and Novitiate

1935-1954

Richard James Novak was born on August 2, 1935, in Johnstown, Pennsylvania, the second son of Michael and Irene Novak. Michael and Irene were first generation American born Slovaks whose parents had fled the Empire of Austria-Hungary between 1870 and 1900. Their parents had reacted to severe Hungarian oppression and the "Magyarisation" movement that had clamped down on the use of the Slovak language and suppressed their culture. Richard's paternal grandmother, Johanna, arrived in NY on the USS Friesland in August 1900 at age 15, and within a year met and married Stephen Novak. Stephen was a Slovak immigrant 15 years her senior, a widower with three children, but he had the necessary U.S. citizenship. He died 10 years later, leaving Johanna a penniless widow with seven children. Nonetheless, Johanna faithfully contributed to Matica Slovenska, a society dedicated to the preservation of the Slovak language and culture, a substitute for national political institutions prohibited by the Kingdom of Hungary.

Father Novak's maternal grandfather Ben Sakmar, who emigrated to avoid being drafted into the Hungarian army, arrived in the USA in December of 1900 at the age of 21. In his 61 years in the US, he used his native language most of the time in order to preserve it. In 1909, he married an American born Slovak, Anna Timchak, in Johnstown, PA.

Ben often told his family that his inheritance to them was the Catholic faith, especially a strong devotion to the crucified Lord, to the holy cross. Before leaving the empire of Austria-Hungary on October 31, 1900, Ben had a tall wooden cross placed near his home in Brutovce on a steep hillside in the Carpathian mountains that overlooked the Spis valley. Later he sent money back to have the cross re-placed with a full metal crucifix enshrined in a wooden frame with a metal fence enclosing the shrine and a small plaque recording his prayer for the safety of his family. It is there to this day, with a stunning view of the snow-capped Tatra Mountains above green expansive valleys. This deep commitment to the Catholic faith through Christ on the cross, and the value and the importance of preserving indigenous culture and language, were to reverberate throughout Richard Novak's life. Michael and Irene learned Slovak from their parents, but chose to only speak and teach English to their growing family.

By 1944 Michael and Richard had two more brothers: James Joseph, born in 1939, and

Richard and Michael Novak, circa 1938.

Benjamin Edward, born in 1943. He was confirmed Richard James Michael Novak by the Most Rev. Hugh C. Boyle at St. Pius Church in McKeesport, PA on May 27, 1947.

In August of 1947, his older brother Michael left home by train for Holy Cross Seminary at Notre Dame, IN, following a cousin who had departed to study for the priesthood at Notre Dame the year before. This brought the whole Novak family into close contact with the Congregation of Holy Cross. It was only natural then that when Richard's grandmother Anna Sakmar suddenly died of a stroke in 1952, Irene asked Michael's superiors at Holy Cross about an appropriate memorial for her mother. When advised that a tabernacle and an altar were needed in East Pakistan for the new Notre Dame College, Irene's father Ben Sakmar agreed to donate the funds for the tabernacle in his wife's name. His three children then donated the altar in their parents' memory, a more fitting tribute than they realized at the time.

Called Nick by his friends and Richie at home, Richard was an honors student at Johnstown Catholic High School, a member of the Student Council, a sports reporter, a literary staff writer, and a member of the orchestra and the band, playing the clarinet. In early 1953, Nick won a competitive examination for a $500.00 Rev. James A. Burns Memorial Scholarship to attend Notre Dame

University in South Bend, Indiana. He planned to take a combined engineering and law program when he entered Notre Dame in September of 1953, immediately enrolling in ROTC and joining the famed marching band.

However, by January 1954, Nick, now known as Dick, decided to join the Holy Cross order and, according to the Holy Cross Eastern Province archives, on February 1, 1954 he entered the seminary at Notre Dame. In June of that year, he elected to join the still new Eastern Province of Holy Cross, which his brother Michael had chosen for his novitiate in 1951. Both Fathers Bob Malone and Jim Denn reported that they and their classmates were disappointed Dick had left the Indiana Province.[1]

Dick Novak entered the newly established Holy Cross Novitiate at Bennington, VT, and on August 15, 1954, he received his holy habit. Many of his classmates at Bennington remember him well. "His classmates loved him," Joe Skaff told me in conversations at Stonehill. Joe explained how he, Dick, Bill Gleason and Jim Donohue started the "Good Neighbors Club", which required them to go around to celebrate a classmate's birthday with

---

[1] Novak, Mary Ann, conversations with Father Bob Malone at Holy Cross Center, North Easton, MA, October 31-November 2, 2007, and with Father James Denn at Holy Cross House, Notre Dame, Indiana, May 4-7, 2008

paper hats, kazoos, and tin drums before the bell for the 5:30AM rising.[2]

Father Bill Condon, after recalling Dick's love of pranks, noted about him in the novitiate: "Dick was a very serious novice, very intense, very spiritual, and kept silence better than most. He was kind, considerate, gentle of others, and engaged in no disputatious fights."

Father Dick Segreve said that "Richard never pushed himself on you; he was a very low key guy. You accepted Dick Novak as Dick Novak or not; he was self-directed, knew where he was going. The essence of Richard Novak was that he was complete, integral. He was a very calm and collected person."

Bill Braun, another fellow novice of Dick's at Bennington, recalled that "his smile is what stands out. He saw through things; he never had a need to get even or prove himself to anyone. He was obedient to the rule, but he saw human kindness and charity as more important than the rule."

It was at Bennington while taking his vows as a religious on August 16, 1955, that Dick first

---

[2] Novak, Mary Ann, conversations with Joe Skaff at Stonehill College Archives; with Father Dick Segreve at Holy Cross Center; with Bill Braun and Father Bill Condon at Holy Cross Family Ministries, North Easton, MA, October 31-November 2, 2007

The Novak family in February 1944, left to right: Irene holding Ben, James, Richard, Michael, and Michael, Sr.

declared his intention to become a missionary, and Father DePrizio, then Provinical Superior of the Eastern Province, asked him to wait another few years until he "was certain enough to fight for the Missions."[3]

In a letter to his family at Easter of 1955, Dick wrote:

"I'm still rather dazed by Dad's totally un-expected visit. It was wonderful to talk to him...

---

[3] Novak, Richard J., C.S.C, letter to Rev. George S. DePrizio, C.S.C., Provincial, 17 September, 1961

"Fr. Evans, C.S.C., one of our India Missionaries, who is from Pittsfield, was here last February. Of course, you're saying, he's the one who talked me into this idea of becoming a missionary. Actually, he didn't, though the example of solid religion and zeal which he gave did much to make me lash into the life. At first I decided to take the vow even though I wasn't too interested in the missions, simply because I wanted to make my vows of obedience complete. But my director said I'd need a positive motive. So I've been reading a lot on the missions, and seeing more and more how much the life would suit me. And I don't consider it as any "dream" I have of baptizing hundreds of pagans that only happens to the pioneers, and the saints, like Francis Xavier. Rather, my life will be more of a pastor's life, taking care of the already-Christians and maybe making a few conversions, but mostly just routine. Maybe I'll be teaching school. There are jobs for hundreds over there, and though only the apostleship among the Garo Hill tribes is anyway 'romantic.' Everything about the place appeals to me, from the weather on up. There are 20 million souls over there, and they're just waiting for me.

"But does this sound so strange to you, that your son should want to be a missionary? What! Don't you realize that this is your reward for your devotion to St. Thérèse? She, who is the patron of the missions, and in a special manner of the missions of Bengal, can reward you in no finer way than to make one of your sons the missionary that she always desired to be. Have you not read in that book on Thérèse's fathers great desire of the Martin family for a boy to send as a missionary?

Does it not seem providential that the priest who confessed me most at Notre Dame, old 'Mike' Matthis is the community's greatest

Father Richard Novak, C.S.C.

promoter of the missions? And that the Carmel of Loretto, so close to home and so well known to you, is one of those dedicated to prayer for the Bengal Mission? And that you should donate the altar in Dacca where, God willing, some day I may say Mass?

"Hello, if you want me to wait three years, I'll wait, but I'll be counting the days till my boat arrives in Goa."

According to his brother James Novak in an introduction to his 1993 book, *Bangladesh: Reflections on the Water*, Dick's announcement caused an unexpected reaction:

"When he announced the [missionary] vow to my father, a strange thing occurred. After we left the Novitiate House in Bennington, Vermont, my father, suddenly and uncharacteristically, pulled our car to the roadside and stopped. Then he cried. Recovering his composure, he told me he had had a vision that had seemed so real: he had seen my brother stabbed. As my father was a man of intuition but not of visions, this demonstration of emotion greatly impressed me..."[4]

---

[4] Novak, James J., "Bangladesh: Reflections on the Water," 1993, Preface, page xiii

II.

Studying at Stonehill
and in France
1955-1961

In September 1955, Dick joined his older brother at Pius X Seminary at Stonehill College for Michael's senior year. Brother Herman Zaccarelli, C.S.C. wrote:

"It is true that Richard Novak's story of love for his fellow men and women was indeed short, but he was a powerful example to me and our community... I lived with Richard and his brother Michael at Pius X Seminary in the early 1950's for approximately two years. During his seminary days, it was his Joy and Peace [sic] that I especially remember. The living situation in the seminary at that time was extremely difficult. I never heard Richard complain about anything. His simplicity of life was evident. He stood out as a seminarian for his peacefulness and his genuine sense of humor. It was apparent to me that his goal was to be a missionary at the service of the poor. He spoke about this with me and others. Richard was always a true example to me that 'God is revealed when we love one another.' The space between Richard's birth and death was a short span of years in which he did love his flock, and he laid down his life for them. I consider him a martyr and a saint."[5]

At Stonehill, Dick was known for his dry, mischievous humor, his bright imagination and his love of the outdoors. He was active in sports and, slight though he was at about 5'11 and 130 lbs,[6] he was well known for being tough, wiry, and playing football smarter than almost anyone else. In his 1958 Stonehill yearbook, and in the living memories of his former classmates, he is credited with being the creator and driving force for via Paludosa, a land bridge and short cut the seminarians built across the boggy fields to the classrooms, allowing them to avoid the 'beltway'

[5] Zaccarelli, Brother Herman E., C.S.C., signed, undated document on letterhead entitled Richard J. Novak, 1935-1964, to Mary Ann Novak, postmarked Orlando, FL, 01 May 2008

[6] Novak, Richard James, Selective Service System Registration Certificate, August 3, 1953

which circled the grounds the long way to Donohue Hall.

Upon graduating *magna cum laude* from Stonehill in 1958, Dick was sent for the summer to lead pilgrimages at the Oratoire Saint-Joseph in Montreal, of which he said in a letter to Father DePrizio:

> "I hope I may become worthy of the honor of wearing the Crucifix, that I may become a worthy religious of Holy Cross. ... [working here] makes us realize the greatness of the Priesthood for which we are preparing. And to desire more that we may use these years of preparation to make us more worthy to 'go unto the altar of God, who gives joy to our youth.'"[7]

Dick was assigned to Le Mans, France, for his theological studies on the recommendation of Superior General Christopher O'Toole.[8]

In a June 15, 1958 letter to his parents, Dick wrote:

> "The reason I'm uncertain about the typewriter, and the reason I didn't go to Boston College this

---

[7] Richard J. Novak, C.S.C., letter to Rev. George S. DePrizio, C.S.C., Provincial Superior, 25 July 1958

[8] O'Toole, Rev. Christopher J., C.S.C., Superior General, letter to Rev. George S. DePrizio, C.S.C., Provinical Superior, May 20, 1958

summer, is that I'll be going to France for my theology. Le Mans. Naturally it came as quite a surprise, and isn't exactly official yet, but pretty certain. Perhaps I mentioned to you that there was some pressure on the Provincial to send a man over, and since I have some French already, and am of a somewhat carefree nature, Father is sending me.

"And of course I'm quite happy about the whole thing. Naturally I would have preferred Rome, where I'd be with Mike, but in France I'll be able to live without Mike having gone before, which

From left to right: Daniel Deveau (Canada), William Norris (Indiana Province), Charles Bodin (France), Claude Richard (France), Gérard Roquet (France), Roger Marchand (France), Jacques Choquette (Canada), local superior, unknown French postulant, Bill Persia (U.S. Eastern Province of Priests), Charlie Stahler (Indiana Province), Richard Novak (U. S. Eastern Province of Priests), Robert Morin (Canada), Archibald Keilen (Indiana Province), Henri Bourgeois (U.S. Eastern Province of Priests).

may or may not be an advantage, but at least it'll be an experience."

On August 16, 1958, Dick made his perpetual profession. But on August 25, he wrote to Fr. DePrizio of his concern that Fr. DePrizio might not send him to France because of Michael's recent decision to return home from Rome, and he reiterated his own desires:

"I am anxious to study theology, and willing to do it wherever I am sent, certain that wherever obedience sends me I will find fulfillment of my vocation... I do not feel that anything which occurs should take away from the dedication of myself which I made the 16th last... I find it constantly necessary in everything I do to reaffirm a decision to be a good Religious and a good Priest..."[9]

On September 14, 1958, Dick sailed to France on the S.S. Homeric from Montreal for his theological studies at the University of d'Angers. On arrival in France, he wrote Father DePrizio:

"If first impressions are the most important, then I should not have troubles at all over here. Of course, a life without troubles would be most

---

[9] Novak, Richard, J., C.S.C., letter to Rev. George DePrizio, C.S.C., Provincial Superior, August 25, 1958

boring, so I'll manage to find some—as soon as I learn the language."[10]

Several people told me that Dick learned the language in remarkably short time, showing his aptitude and respect for indigenous languages. Pere Daniel Deveau wrote in January 2008:

"I remember him as a quiet and peaceful young man, more on the intellectual side than the usual American seminarian. He loved to discuss ideas and concepts. He also was a man of prayer, and he led a simple life... he learned the language very early. I considered him as a very bright mind."[11]

After describing a mission in Mers-les-Mains in the summer of 1960, Dick showed his love for France in a letter to Father DePrizio:

"It was a good and deep experience, Father, and thus extremely hard to describe. But it sure was delicious to live among the Frenchmen, and have the occasion to see their manner of living and thinking."[12]

---

[10] Novak, Richard J., C.S.C, letter to Father George S. DePrizio, C.S.C., Provincial Superior, 8 October, 1958

[11] Deveau, Pere Daniel, C.S.C., District Superior, District d'Acadie, letter to Mary Ann Novak, January 8, 2008

[12] Novak, Richard, C.S.C., letter to Rev. George DePrizio, C.S.C., Provincial Superior, 6 August 1960

Dick also arranged for bicycles for all the seminarians and led them on weekend and mission trips throughout France. Father Bill Persia, C.S.C., a fellow seminarian in Le Mans, said of Dick:

"He was the lone American sent to Le Mans following graduation in 1958; he provided care and concern for all of us that followed, and led reconstruction of the living quarters: installing showers, and a new furnace. Dick translated notes so that we could study, and ordered English books for the library. He convinced Pere Gagnon to buy us bicycles so we could travel, and he traced out a plan of action for all our trips, wrote to different seminaries to arrange for us to stay there, just had everything set up in advance. Richard had a great simplicity, even in the way he dressed, no errors in his appearance. He didn't flaunt his intelligence, but was always analyzing and looking ahead: he was visionary, way ahead of Rome, even as they were preparing for Vatican II. He used beautiful liturgies and songs. Dick was not afraid to express his opinions; if he thought something was right, he said so, even if it was far out or might offend someone: The truth was the truth. He was straightforward, and people admired him for that. He couldn't sit by and do nothing, ever."[13]

---

[13] Persia, Rev. William, C.S.C., conversation with Mary Ann Novak, Holy Cross Family Ministries, November 1, 2007

"Have bike and beret; will travel."

Dick's ability to immerse himself in the culture was evident in his travels through the countryside that he described in his many letters to Father George DePrizio. Dick adopted the French beret and noted in an October newsletter entitled French Follies '58: "Have bike and beret; will travel." Dick is pictured on bended knee in front of his fellow seminarians on a trip in 1959.[14] In a November 1960 letter to his parents, Dick wrote: "I am thinking seriously of taking the vow for the foreign missions. I don't plan to take it before returning to

---

[14] Richard Novak with classmates in France, 1959, picture courtesy of Pere Daniel Deveau, C.S.C.

Archbishop Lawrence Graner, C.S.C. at the ordination of Father Richard Novak, C.S.C., Notre Dame de Sainte Croix, Le Mans, June 29, 1961.

the States, but I thought I'd mention it to get you used to the idea. I think I could be more useful in one of our missions than I would be back in the States."

In the spring of 1961, he received his S.T.B. *cum laude*. His ordination that June is memorable for several unusual reasons, in addition to the obvious attainment of his sacred priesthood. For one, he was scheduled to be ordained with great pomp and ceremony with the French seminarians by Archbishop Chevalier of Le Mans at the 11th century Cathedral of St. Julien at 8:30 AM on June 29, 1961. The invitations were all printed that, including those for his First Mass to be held in

Johnstown, PA, in August. Instead, at the last minute, when he heard that Archbishop Lawrence Graner, C.S.C., of Dacca 'and the Indes Orientales', as the local paper in Le Mans noted, would be passing through Le Mans on that day, he asked permission to be ordained by him, symbolic of his commitment to the missions.

Permission granted, he was ordained alone 'in all simplicity,' as a French paper reported, in Notre Dame de Sainte Croix at 9AM on June 29, 1961, the solemnity of Saints Peter and Paul. Father George DePrizio, his Provinical Superior, Pere Gagnon, his parents Michael and Irene, and a dozen of Dick's seminarian friends, were present.

Father Richard Novak's ordination.

The second reason Dick Novak's ordination is so memorable is that Archbishop Graner tripped while descending to distribute communion and the Holy Hosts scattered across the altar steps. Even then superstitions were whispered, and this event was recalled by many upon news of his death, including by Fr. Bartley MacPhaidin, C.S.C., in a verse of a poem he wrote dedicated to Father Novak:

Who could have told nine hundred days ago
White priest, gathering white hosts,
That God would ask your Christ-life to unite
The dusky host of thousands dying with you
And value with your own the Orient-rich life
Asked by the Prophet's holy hair[15]

While in France, Dick continued to consider taking the fourth vow, recognized as the missionary vow, "discussing it with the Director in France from the 1st year on."[16] While assigned to Washington following his ordination in 1961, he wrote in the same letter to Father DePrizio: "Although I have not spoken of the Missions for three years, the thought of this apostolate has not been far from my mind during this time." This time his request for the foreign mission was approved, and he was assigned

---

[15] MacPhaidin, Rev Bartley, C.S.C., "For Richard Novak My brother-priest in Holy Cross", final verse, 1964

[16] Novak, Rev. Richard , C.S.C. letter to Rev. George S. DePrizio, C.S.C., Provincial Superior, 17 September 1961

to the Foreign Mission Society under Father Arnold Fell, C.S.C.[17] He wrote his parents on September 26th:

"The reason I wanted you down was to tell you that I shall be moving up the Foreign Mission Seminary soon. All has been arranged this past week. From the looks of things, I shall be studying Arabic this year, and if all goes well, I shall begin to study Islamic culture. I didn't want to have to write about it, preferring to talk about it with you, but things moved a lot faster than normal, and here I am. It really is the greatest thing that ever happened to the Missions because they have never had anyone who had studied Islam and the Mohammedans over in [East] Pakistan. It will, however, if it goes through, mean a lot of years of study before I get over to Pakistan."

By October 1st, Father Dick Novak had reported to the Foreign Mission Seminary in Washington, DC, where he chose to be the first Holy Cross priest to study Arabic and Islam in a systematic way, to support Christianity's earliest dialogue with Islam, to become an interlocutor between the two religions. He hoped to find a bridge between the two religions, with the idea of continuing the dialogue which St. Thomas Aquinas had begun in

---

[17] DePrizio, Rev. George, C.S.C., Provincial Superior, letter to Father Richard Novak, C.S.C, September 29, 1961

his *Summa Contra Gentiles* nearly seven centuries earlier. In the process, he fell in love with Bengal and the study of Arabic, and was strengthened in his strong desire to become a world-class expert on Moslem and Christian relations. In this alone, he was seen as a model for many of the young Holy Cross seminarians. The late Father Richard Mazziotta, C.S.C. noted in a January 1994 Memorial Liturgy for Father Novak, held only a few months

Father Richard Novak with Mary Ann Novak in Johnstown, PA after returning from France.

before his own premature death, that twenty-five years earlier:

"We seminarians often spoke about Father Novak. As the first priest to study Arabian philosophy, he seemed the epitome of the new Catholic missionary, one fully immersed in another culture, and someone sympathetic to a different religion. Struck down by the same people who were the subject of his openness, he seemed the prototypical imitator of Christ, a priest whose life and passage schooled us in what ministry and witness would mean in the open Church of Vatican II."[18]

It is clear from the letters found in the various Archives that Fathers DePrizio and Fell had a program in mind for Father Novak, which certainly entailed his beginning his desired Islamic studies, but their long range plans for achieving the program weren't fully revealed. While Father Novak joined the American Friends of the Middle East organization, Father Fell writes Fr. DePrizio on September 22, 1961:

"Your telephone call the other day concerning the assignment of Father Richard Novak took my breath away, and perhaps I was not responding with

---

[18] Mazziotta, Rev. Richard, C.S.C., Sermon for the Memorial Liturgy: Father Richard J. Novak, C.S.C., given at the Chapel of Mary, Stonehill College, North Easton, MA, January 21, 1994

the normal reflexes. I called him and informed him of the decision, after talking it over with Father Harrington, and advised him to say nothing about it until you had written Father Bernard. He was, of course, quite elated with the assignment. ... If he is to emphasize Islamic studies, it will be necessary for him to begin some study of Arabic immediately."[19]

On September 30th, Father DePrizio responded to Father Fell:

"Father Novak is an excellent worker and has a strong intelligence. He should be able to do well in specialized language study as well as missiological studies. I think this is a good opportunity for you to develop one of those specialists that you have frequently spoken about."[20]

On October 2nd, Father Fell outlined an immediate course of study for Father Novak, beginning with an initial study of Arabic at Harvard, and a course in Cultural Anthropology, recommended by Dr. Frank of the Department of Semitic Languages at Catholic University. But he notes in his letter his concerns about Father Novak:

---

[19] Fell, Rev. Arnold A., C.S.C., Director, Holy Cross Missions, letter to Rev. George DePrizio, C.S.C., Provincial Superior, September 22, 1961

[20] DePrizio, Rev. George, C.S.C., Provincial Superior, letter to Father Arnold Fell, C.S.C., Director, Holy Cross Missions, September 30, 1961

"It was necessary for him to register quickly, and we told him to do so, presuming that the course outlined would meet your approval. ... This is not, as I am sure you know, an easy field he is choosing, and he will certainly need to be the excellent worker and strong intelligence that you described him to be."[21]

Father DePrizio responds quickly with approval on October 5th:

"The Program you have outlined for Father Novak seems excellent. Be sure that whatever you decide for him to do and study meets with my full approval. As far as I am concerned he is entirely in your hands. Although the program will be a great challenge, I am certain that Father Novak will respond to it well. So far as I know he is a good worker and will keep at it faithfully."[22]

Thus, Father Novak began his course of studies at Catholic University, and made his Foreign Mission vow on February 2, 1962 in the chapel of the Holy Cross Foreign Mission Seminary, completing the Special Missiology Program in May of 1962. He

[21] Fell, Rev. Arnold A., C.S.C., Director, Holy Cross Missions, letter to Rev. George DePrizio, C.S.C., Provincial Superior, October 2, 1961

[22] DePrizio, Rev. George, C.S.C., Provincial Superior, letter to Rev. Arnold A. Fell, C.S.C., Director, Holy Cross Missions, October 5, 1961

spent the summer of 1962 at Harvard University studying Arabic as planned. He was then assigned to the Oriental Institute in Barisal, East Pakistan, for the study of the Bengali language, and the study of the culture and history of the Bengali people.

Before leaving for his new assignment, Father Dick Novak and his brother Michael came to their parent's home in Johnstown, PA, on September 1, 1962 for a few weeks visit, and Karen Laub, later to

Father Richard Novak with parents and siblings in Johnstown, PA before leaving for East Pakistan.

become Michael's wife, stopped to say goodbye on her return to Cambridge.

I recall Richard as cheerful and fun, sweet and lovable, and our family photo of his departure show his good cheer. Memories of him are almost always humorous, light-hearted, life-affirming. He was funny and cool, taping the popular songs off the radio one summer evening in before he left, songs like "Poison Ivy" by The Coasters, Bobby Darin's "Splish Splash" and James Brown's "Do the Mashed Potatoes", singing along with the tape, joking all the time about dancing in East Pakistan, and I just thought him the coolest brother anyone could have. He later wrote me from East Pakistan about listening to some of those songs there. After all, what did I know of East Pakistan? I assumed he would be laughing and joking, singing and dancing over there too, and he wrote me of crashing a wedding and other funny stories which suggested he was having a fun time there.

III.

Life as a Missionary in East Pakistan
1962-1963

In October 1962, he left the United States for the last time, traveling to Lebanon for ten days on his way over to visit with the extended family of Joe Skaff. The Johnstown *Tribune-Democrat* printed the following, in part, in October 1962:

Young Priest Going to East Pakistan

"A former Westmont resident is en route to the Far East to begin a 2 to 5-year course of advanced study and work with the Holy Cross Fathers there.

"He is the Rev. Richard James Novak, CSC, son of Mr. and Mrs. Michael J. Novak of 1435

Paulton Street, who is scheduled to arrive in Dacca, East Pakistan, Tuesday.

"Upon arrival in East Pakistan, the young priest will enroll at the Oriental Institute at Barisal to begin a year's study of the language, culture, history, art and customs of the Bengali peoples.

"Following his studies, he will teach at Notre Dame College in Dacca and do missionary field work.

"Father Novak was ordained in June 1961 in Le Mans, France, after his graduation from the Universite D'Angers at Angers, France, where he received a degree in sacred theology.

"Following his ordination, Father Novak returned to the United States to continue studies in theology, mission work and cultural anthropology at Catholic University, Washington, D.C.

"Last summer he studied Arabic at Harvard University under a scholarship from the inter-university program of Middle East studies.

"Father Novak left the States Oct. 1, with stopovers scheduled for Rome, Italy; Beirut, Lebanon; Damascus, Syria; Jordan and the Holy Land."

In November, Father DePrizio wrote to Father Novak on his trip:

"I enjoyed hugely your description of the ten days spent in Lebanon. That paragraph of your letter should be amplified into a monograph ... You have this great blessing of being able to draw readily from every facet of your experiences—spiritual, temporal, cultural."[23]

Father Novak arrived in Barisal on November 1, 1962, and soon found that during studies there, he was bored by being kept indoors in classes and asked to be released,[24] when he promptly joined the third-grade boys in their classes at Kishore Primary School in Barisal—'after falling behind the fifth graders', he joked in a Pakistan Letter.[25] Then, Father Novak was sent to Dacca to be an instructor in logic at Notre Dame College.

One of his first acts in Dacca was celebrating Mass on the altar donated in honor of his grandparents. "We were so happy when Richard told us he was there saying mass on it ... at Notre Dame College. Back in '52 or '53 we never expected

---

[23] DePrizio, Rev. George, C.S.C., Provincial Superior, letter to Rev. Richard Novak, C.S.C., November 10, 1962

[24] Novak, Father Richard, C.S.C, letter to Rev. Arnold Fell, C.S.C., Director, Holy Cross Missions, January 23, 1963

[25] Pakistan Letters, undated

a son of ours to say Mass at that particular altar! Dacca seemed so remote."[26] Irene Novak wrote to Fathers DePrizio and McKee.

In October of 1962, Dick received a letter from Wilson Bishai, an Assistant Professor of Middle East Studies at the Johns Hopkins School of Advanced International Studies, commenting very favorably on the research potential in an essay Dick had sent him about "the clash between Israel and Canaan," and referring to a visit Dick had had with them and wishing him "the Lord's blessing as you serve him in East Pakistan."[27]

Dick had a deep interest in the Bengali people, culture and language, and, as Fr. Gus Peverada noted in his vignette on Father Novak, "He would often visit local families and he was frequently seen at the Tejgaon Bottomley Home Orphanage, where he loved to play with the children and practice his Bengali with them. He slept on a native chowki and often wore the chaddar…" An excerpt from a letter to his parents on June 15, 1963:

"We were all trapped for a few days at the mission because the storm made the rivers on either side of the mission impassable. While

[26] Novak, Irene, letters to Rev. George DePrizio, C.S.C., February 11th and to Rev. Robert McKee, February 15, 1964

[27] Bishai, Wilson, letter to Father Richard Novak, C.S.C., October 8, 1962

there I studied Bengali, practiced it with the patients and with the nurses, went hunting for moneys with the Pastor because these herds of monkeys were invading the pineapple gardens and eating up all those wonderful fruits. Then when the river subsided I waded across and went across the paddy fields about nine miles to the next mission, Mariamnagor (translation: Mary's city). From there I accompanied a father to a distant mission in the hills, about 15 miles. We slept on straw mats in a little bamboo hut, ate our rice and curry with fingers. They made us tea, but since they didn't have any sugar they decided the next best thing was salt. They never drink tea themselves so they didn't know what an obnoxious drink they were serving to a couple of really dry and thirsty men. We drank it —and then asked for another cup, assuring them that we really could drink tea without sugar or salt. Returning to Mariamnagor the next day I found a letter saying return to Dacca at once. Well the letter was ten days old so I didn't exactly get to Dacca "at once". But in the morning I set out on bike, waded to a river, walked about a mile in knee deep mud carrying the bike, took a ferry at one place, rode the bike about two miles, gave it to a Catholic to take back to the mission, took a rickshaw for eight miles, then a bus another eight, then another ferry, walked about two miles, and finally got a train to Mymensingh, where my clothes were. Picking them up and grabbing some rice and curry, I got another train an hour later and arrived in Dacca at 8 PM last eve, where I read my mail and found out I didn't really have to come to Dacca at all."

A fellow Holy Cross missionary, Fr. George Pope, noted that he had met Dick Novak the first time briefly while visiting a friend in LeMans in November 1958, but did not have any opportunity to get to know him. Then in the summer of 1963, while spending a month in Shillong on vacation, Dick joined them for some period of time. Fr. Pope and Dick went to the movie together to see a film of some import, perhaps Dr. Zhivago, and they spent some time afterwards talking about it. His observations of Dick were that "he was quiet, composed, kind, self-confident, perceptive of people, intuitive, and intelligent. He was very motivated, especially towards creating a bridge to Islamic culture. He was ahead of his times..." "Dick took long walks alone," Fr. Pope said, and "I believe that at least a secondary feature of those singular walks was that he wanted to get acquainted with the people in the country, wanted to meet them and talk with them."

Father Richard Timm, C.S.C., wrote of Father Novak:

"He was very friendly and likeable and showed his unmistakable interest in people. The kids at the orphanage loved him and liked to play and converse with him. He got around to more places than most of our men who have been here for many years. People everywhere still remember him. I used to worry about him, though, because it seemed to me that his liberal spirit was liable to get him into trouble sooner or later."[28]

In a letter to his parents in January 1963, Father Novak stated that, "I just learned that I shall probably spend 2 years at ND College in Dacca after I finish my year here, and then, if plans continue, should go to Montreal for studies. There is talk about attending a summer school in Morocco, but that's still vague yet."[29] This uncertainty remained in the background for all of them.

Father Fell was clearly working from a plan for Father Richard, and he wrote Father Richard in February 1963:

"Incidentally, and I know you understand that this and much of the rest I write you is confidential (nothing like being quoted overseas

---

[28] Timm, Rev. Richard W., C.S.C., letter to Mary Ann Novak, February 6, 1966

[29] Novak, Rev. Richard J., C.S.C., letter to Michael J and Irene Novak, 24 January 1963

to raise the hackles). I recently wrote to Father McKee again and reminded him that I did not want you put into definite work under ecclesiastical authority but rather in a Community house, i.e., the College or Moreau House. I would have no objection to your teaching, or taking courses in your line at Dacca University, but with some consideration of your having some time to visit other parts of the mission and soak up as much knowledge of the mission operation as possible. This before returning to this country or elsewhere for further studies in Islamics. Just how long you should stay over there this time cannot be specifically determined right now. Maybe a year, a year-and-a-half, or two years. Perhaps you would need the latter period to really absorb some of the mission life and flavor. I also mentioned to him that if he could not so base you (and I do not see why not) in a Community house, then to send you back home."[30]

Some correspondence suggests that the plan was to bring him back quickly for advanced studies, likely within the year. In June, Father Novak told Father Fell that he was "awaiting a meeting of the Equivalence Committee at Dacca U to see if I can go

---

[30] Fell, Rev. Arnold A., C.S.C, Director, Holy Cross Missions, letter to Rev. Richard Novak, C.S.C., February 25, 1963

for the M.A. in one year."[31] Instead, the word came back, he wrote Father DePrizio in August, that "... the final decision was that it will take two years. I would not have to go to class; merely to appear for the final exams; but since I am not sure how long Fr. Fell and yourself are going to leave me over here, I don't know whether two years will be soon enough."[32]

He began work on a Masters in September 1963 although Father Fell did not give his final approval that he could stay the full term, despite strong pleading by Father Novak. He gained many admirers while studying at Dacca University, including Dr. Ghani, Vice-Chancellor of Dacca University, Dr. Habibullah, Head of the Department of Islamic History, and Dr. Rahman, Provost of Dacca Hall.

Dick was admitted to the Bengali Academy and the Asiatic Society of Dacca in 1963,[33] one of the first Americans to be admitted. He noted that he was translating from the French a work from the Sorbonne on Bengali phonetics.

---

[31] Novak, Rev. Richard, C.S.C., letter to Rev. Arnold Fell, C.S.C., Director, Holy Cross Missions, 17 June 1963

[32] Novak, Rev. Richard, C.S.C., letter to Rev. George DePrizio, C.S.C., Provincial Superior, 21 August 1963

[33] Ibid.

IV.

Death in East Pakistan
1964

The entire decade of the 1960s was marked by great ferment in East Pakistan as this Bengal province sought to define its identity within the larger Moslem state. "Trouble had been brewing between East and West Pakistan since their union in 1947, which was based solely on the fact that East Pakistan was predominantly Moslem," as Father Richard W. Timm, C.S.C., noted, "and many felt that such an unwieldy combination based solely on a common religion, would not last long."[34]

Separated from West Pakistan by almost one thousand miles of Indian territory, East Pakistan was

---

[34] Timm, Richard W., C.S.C., "150 Years of Holy Cross in East Bengal Mission," Congregation of Holy Cross, Dhaka, 2003, pg 66

essentially a Bengali Province in both language and culture, whereas West Pakistan spoke several languages including Urdu. There was considerable turmoil in East Pakistan when it was commanded by the government in Islamabad to adopt Urdu as its language and to alter its culture in the 1950s. By the 1960s Syed Abid Hussain, a former Vice Chancellor of Jamia Millia Islamia stated quite frankly in his 1965 book *The Destiny of Indian Muslims*:

> "There has been a re-emergence of Muslim communalism. This is, as a matter of fact, the same movement of religious communalism which had started shortly before 1947, had temporarily subsided after partition and is now coming to the surface again. It is sponsored by a small section of religious leaders but is becoming fairly popular among the middle class and to some extent among students."[35]

Thus, in these days Muslim riots were easily set off against the long-settled Hindu minority, and such was the case in January 1964 when the theft of a Muslim relic—the "Prophet's holy hair" in Father MacPhaidin's poem—at Srinagar in Kashmir triggered ferocious Muslim attacks against Hindus in East Pakistan when over 29 people were killed. This event sparked retaliation where over 100 were

---

[35] Quoted in the Organiser, August 17, 2003

killed by January 13th, and from there the riots spread. Holy Family Hospital in Dacca was operated by the Catholic Medical Missionaries, and its 100 beds were crowded with victims of the riots in those early days of January 1964. These were sights and conditions that greatly disturbed Father Novak as he traveled around Dacca on his bike on January 15, Sister Lourdes reported to Father McKee.[36] According to Sister Mary Lourdes, Administrator of the Holy Family Hospital, "Fr. Novak came on several occasions [during the riots] to ask if he could help as we brought in the wounded. He was distraught at the sights on the street."[37] Sister Angela, Superior of the Medical Mission Missionaries, wrote of Father Novak: "He could know no rest because he wanted to become personally involved in the suffering of the people."[38]

A U.S. Government report from Washington dated January 16, 1964, in the Lyndon B. Johnson Presidential Papers, states:

---

[36] McKee, Rev. Robert, C.S.C., "Fr. Novak Case–His Contact with Holy Family Hospital" as learned from Sister Lourdes, Superintendent of Holy Family Hospital, January 15th and 16th, 1964

[37] Cody, Loretta, formerly Sister Mary Lourdes, Life's A Story, An Autobiography, second edition, 2007, page 53

[38] Sister Mary Angela, Holy Family Hospital, letter to Rev. Robert McKee, C.S.C., January 25, 1964

"The major scene of the Hindu-Muslim rioting has shifted to Pakistan at Narayanganj, a few miles south of Dacca in East Pakistan, a minimum of 300 Hindus were killed on January 13-14. ... One such demonstration in Khulna, East Pakistan, deteriorated into anti-Hindu riots in which at least 27 persons died. A factor which undoubtedly contributed to the atmosphere in which these riots took place was the Indian policy of expulsion from Assam of Muslim immigrants from East Pakistan. [Pakistani] President Ayub, in a strong letter sent to [Indian] President Radhakrishnan January 13, said that already 20,000 Indian Muslims had crossed into East Pakistan since the Calcutta riots began. There are still 10 million Hindus in East Pakistan and over 44 million Muslims in India."[39]

The turmoil in Dacca and environs resulted in the imposition of martial law in the area, but as is often the case, it restricts all but those with the worst intentions. This is the environment in which Father Novak went suddenly missing in January 1964. For many years, the details were unknown to the family, and many of those I have learned are

---

[39] Memorandum From the Executive Secretary of the Department of State (Read) to the President's Special Assistant for National Security Affairs (Bundy) Source: Johnson Library, National Security File, Country File, Pakistan, Vol. I, Memos, 11/63-5/64. Confidential

shocking. The following pages summarize what I have been able to piece together, resolving many but not all my questions.

Father Novak had visited the Holy Family Hospital to see how he could help several times on January 15th, and had been turned away. Late on the evening of January 15th, Sister Mary Lourdes asked Sister Maria Goretti to call Father Novak the next morning and ask if he would help locate the family of a student nurse at Holy Family hospital as she could get no word of her father who worked at the Dhakeshwari Cotton Mills nor of any of her family. When contacted that next morning, Father Novak immediately offered to call or go to Narayanganj to enquire about them.[40]

On January 16, 1964, Father John Vanden-Bossche was acting for Father Eugene Burke, Superior of Notre Dame College, who was traveling with Father Robert McKee, the Dacca District Superior, to Bandhura. Father Novak came to him early that morning and told him of the call from Holy Family Hospital asking him to help locate the Hindu family of the student nurse at the jute mills near Naranyanganj. "He informed me that he was going to go looking for them, having had no success

---

[40] Cody, Loretta, formerly Sr. Mary Lourdes, conversations with Mary Ann Novak, January 2, 2008, and a document from Patricia Traveline, formerly Sr. Maria Goretti, December 28, 2007

on the phone. I gave him my permission, but made him promise he wouldn't cross the river. What could I do?" Father VandenBossche said to me, "I couldn't stop him from going."[41]

On that same morning of January 16th, Sister Mary Lourdes said she arrived early at Notre Dame College in an ambulance to pick up Father Bill Graham on an emergency errand, when Father Novak came out dressed in his white cassock, full black trousers, and a light blue jacket. Father Novak stopped to speak to Sister Lourdes through the back seat window, and he confirmed that Sister Maria Goretti had called him and that he was leaving to make enquiries about the nurse's family. He then spoke briefly to Father Graham in the front seat, according to Sister Lourdes, got on his bicycle and pedaled away while they left on their own emergency errand.[42]

When Fathers McKee and Burke returned to the College that evening of the 16th and learned that Father Novak was missing, they began to search for him. "In the afternoon [of January 16th]," Father VandenBossche indicated, "I went to Comilla to replace Father Dan Kennerk, and I didn't know he

---

[41] VandenBossche, Rev. John, C.S.C., conversations with Mary Ann Novak., Indiana Province Archives, May 5, 2008

[42] Novak, Mary Ann, conversations with Loretta Cody, op cit, confirmed by notes of Rev. McKee, undated, but reversing who Father Novak spoke to first in the ambulance that morning

The Shitalakhya River.

was missing until Father Burke called me late that evening enquiring into Father Novak's whereabouts. I told him what I knew at that time."[43]

For Fathers McKee, Burke, and Graham and the Holy Cross community in Dacca, the next two weeks were suspenseful, stressful and uncharted territory. The day-by-day details are extremely intricate, grotesque and riveting. They spent each day searching the Narayanganj area with police escorts, walking miles to villages, crossing and recrossing the river, and investigating hundreds of corpses: "All

---

[43] VandenBossche, Rev. John, C.S.C., conversation with Mary Ann Novak, op cit

the bodies were bloated, distorted and practically naked."[44]

The Notre Dame Chronicles in Dacca on January 22, 1964, indicate that the search party found "a Pharmacist who identified without a doubt Father Novak, who stopped there for directions at about 10AM, giving them a definite positive lead for Fatullah."[45]

That same day they also made an assessment that "they could not establish that a man like Father Novak actually crossed the river." The only definite facts of all searches so far:

1. Pharmacist at Fatullah at about 10 AM directed Father Novak to Narayanganj, on January 16, 1964.

2. Father Novak spoke to Msgr. D'Costa at St. Paul's Church, Narayanganj, about 11:00 AM on the 16th January, 1964.

3. Father Novak was at Luxmi Narayan Mills at about 1:00 PM on the 16th January, 1964 and went to the ferry ghat.[46]

---

[44] Notre Dame Chronicles, Vol III, Father Novak Search, 20 January 1964, Page One

[45] Notre Dame Chronicles, Search Report–January 22, 1964, Sheet One

[46] Ibid, Sheet One and Two

It was not until January 24th, eight days after Father Novak disappeared, that a witness by the name of Ashraful Huq came to the College. He reported that his maidservant saw the murder of Father Novak occur sometime after 1300 hours by five men, whose names were known. Father Novak was on a boat coming across the Sitalakhya River when, near the landing, he was attacked by two youths on board. When he struggled, the youths called out for others to come and "kill another Hindu." Huq was able to offer vivid details from his maidservant about Father Novak's last moments:

> "He reached for his cross which he wore about his neck and held it out to them, saying 'I am a Christian.' He spoke in Bengali to the youths. But they paid him no heed. Three new youths responding to the calls as the boat docked helped overcome him, dragged him ashore, and while four youths held Father Novak down, one of those on shore named Yunus had a sword, and he stabbed Father Novak twice in the neck and chest, and he died rapidly."[47]

Other witnesses testified to the enormous amount of blood from the stab wounds, according to the Chronicle Records. The Holy Cross search party had in fact stood on the spot near Fatullah where Father Novak was murdered at several times

---

[47] Ibid.

during the investigation, and saw the blood-stained area, but did not know at that time that it was where Father Novak had died. Partly to spare Father Novak's mother the gory details, Father McKee, whose meticulous reports on these events make gripping reading, did not write all the details he knew to the Novak family. But he did advise them and Father Novak's superiors in the US that, even though Father Novak's body had not yet been located, he was "morally certain" they should go ahead with the requiem Masses in North Easton and Dacca on January 27th.

Only on January 29th were the searchers informed that the police had captured the actual murderer, named Yunus, who confessed to stabbing Fr. Novak, and that they were in possession of Father Novak's cycle, watch and glasses:

> "At the Narayanganj police station, Father Burke saw Father Novak's watch, glasses, and cycle and positively identified them beyond any doubt. ... Yunus was brought in chained or tied to another man who was very dark and is said to be one of the men who assisted in throwing Father Novak's body into the river. There was no exchange of words between us."[48]

---

[48] Notre Dame Chronicles, Novak Case–Identification of his effects, January 29, 1964, ibid

Thus, two days after the formal requiem masses were held in Dacca, in North Easton, MA, and in Johnstown, PA, the intensive search for Father Novak ended in East Pakistan.

On January 30, the American Consulate General in Dacca, Pakistan, filed a "Final Report of the Death of an American Citizen" with the State Department in Washington. Not long after this report, the newly elevated President of the United States, Lyndon B. Johnson, called Michael and Irene Novak to express his condolences on the murder of their 28-year-old son, Father Richard Novak, C.S.C.

While Father Novak's parents were kept informed of the search for their son by various representatives of the U.S. Department of State as

Father Robert McKee at the site
of Father Richard Novak's death.

well as the Superior of Holy Cross, they still lacked a full and detailed understanding of what happened to their son. On February 4, 1964, Michael J. Novak Sr. wrote to Father McKee a plea for more information:

"Dear Rev. Father,

"We have been waiting daily for a letter detailing to us all that has happened to our Son, Father Richard Novak. Amidst conflicting reports from the State Department and from news dispatches we would like to know the answers.

"The story we have been able to piece together is this, that on Thur. Jan 16 Richard left on his bicycle to see if Father Costa was alright following the riots in his neighborhood on Tues. preceding. On his way there on the river bank he met a crowd who were looking at a cotton mill on the other side and asked what was over there and that he was told that Hindus were taking refuge in the cotton mill. He mentioned that he was going over to see if he could be of help. And that after reaching there, and when the Hindus were leaving, trying to escape, they were being robbed and beaten, that he remonstrated with the people who were robbing and beating the Hindus to stop, he himself was set upon and killed.

"If this is not so, please tell us the exact truth as we would rather know the truth.

"The news dispatches say that he was stabbed to death resisting thugs who attempted to rob him. We have waited two weeks and now we feel we should write to ask. If your letter is on its way already it will help to ease us."

As it turns out, his letter crossed with the first detailed report from Fr. McKee, dated January 30, 1964, whereby he delineates the known facts following Father Novak to the spot on the river bank where he could board a public ferry, as well as those reports which he has not been able to substantiate: his traversing the river, about the attacks on him at the ferry pier, and about his bicycle, wrist watch, and glasses being taken by the attackers. The search, he explains, is both thorough and professionally conducted.

Nevertheless, Father Richard's father phones Fr. George De Prizio on February 19th, and on the 20th, Fr. DePrizio writes: "I have known for some days that dreadful aftermath of the tragedy. It was communicated to me by the State Department, but I did not inform you because I wanted to spare you and especially Mrs. Novak additional grief."

"In communicating to me the official news of his death," Fr. DePrizio continued, "the report stated that the body was unrecoverable because it was destroyed by dogs and vultures before the Consular Official could get to it. That is the dreadful truth and I have no other details."

Indeed, the rationale for holding back the details is disclosed in the next and concluding paragraph:

"May you use your own discretion and judgment as to whether or not this fact should be communicated to Mrs. Novak. It would seem to me in all charity that a mother should be spared this point. Her grief is already so great."

Nevertheless, when they learned that Father Novak's killers had been apprehended, his parents appealed for leniency, claiming there had been enough suffering and pain already. In a decision issued on October 3, 1964, the trial court in Dacca nevertheless sentenced the man who had stabbed Fr. Novak to death by hanging and sentenced the four others to serve life imprisonment.

On December 22, 1964, the Dacca High Court confirmed the death sentence passed on Yunus Ali on appeal and, on its own motion to the four other accused to show cause why they should not also get the extreme penalty of law, sentenced all five persons to death on the charge of killing Father Novak. Mr. Justice B. A. Siddiky in issuing the judgment "observed that it was a coldblooded

Father Richard Novak's chalice.

murder and that the offence was proved beyond reasonable doubt."[49]

In May of 1966, the Supreme Court of Pakistan confirmed the death sentence passed on Yunus Ali who had "killed Father Novak an American missionary by dagger blows,"[50] and the Court reinstated the original life sentences for the other four. Father McKee ordered and had placed a marble memorial stone at the 17th century Tejgaon

[49] The Pakistan Observer, Dacca, "Father Novak Murder Case: Five to Die," December 23, 1964

[50] The Pakistan Observer, Dacca, "Father Novak Murder Case: One to Die, 4 get life term," May 13, 1966

Holy Rosary Church on January 4, 1966, at a cost of 258 rupees.[51]

Father Novak's beautiful chalice, made in France with the melted down gold and silver of his parents' wedding rings and other family jewelry, is preserved and used for daily Mass at the Holy Cross chapel in North Easton, MA. It has been used by the priests in Father Novak's memory since Father Joseph Lehane, C.S.C. brought it back from Dhaka in 2001.

---

[51] Novak, Father Richard, C.S.C, files, Eastern Province Archives, copy of invoice paid by Father McKee, Dacca

V.

Remembrances and Reminders

In all, Father Novak spent over one third of his life as a member of the Holy Cross Congregation, some ten years. Though he served as missionary for just fifteen months, he made a strong impression on people, and the lasting effects of his work are still remembered. He is remembered as a scholar and as a model by Holy Cross seminarians and priests in the 44 years since his death.

In his moving funeral eulogy (included in full in the Appendix) on January 27, 1964, in Johnstown, PA, Fr. Fell wrote:

> "He was one of the most fearless young men I ever met, and one of the most selfless, which combined to make him most adaptable for the work of a missionary. He was constantly looking for an outstanding challenge and he found it in

his decision to dedicate his life to the apostolate to the Moslems, admittedly one of the most difficult of all apostolate. In twelve hundred years Christianity has never really built a bridge to Islam. Yet, that is what Dick chose, and went off unquestioningly, fearlessly and selflessly to Pakistan."

In recently contemplating Father Novak's life, Father Ernest J. Bartell, C.S.C. said:

"Fr. Fell had a plan for Richard—we all did. We surely miss the many contributions Richard would have made to our Holy Cross global ministries. He brought a clear perspective on the faith we shared that enriched our commitment to mission. Richard would have used his intellectual abilities to enlarge and integrate our understanding and relations with other cultures, perhaps especially with respect to Islam. Richard would have been a leader for Holy Cross in developing a musicology to meet the needs of today's Church.[52]

Father Germain-Marie Lalande, Superior General of Holy Cross, wrote on January 27, 1964, to Father Robert McKee in Dacca:

---

[52] Bartell, Rev. Ernest J., C.S.C., conversation with Mary Ann Novak, Corby Hall, Notre Dame University, May 4, 2008, confirmed in an email to Mary Ann Novak, May 20, 2008

"In the course of a private audience with the Holy Father [Pope John the XXIII], I informed the Holy Father of your great trial. The Holy Father's immediate reaction was: martyrdom. As you can well understand, the nature and reasons for Father Novak's death will have to be ascertained before we can speak of martyrdom... This is God's mysterious way of building up His Church..."

Fr. Germain Lalande, in telling Pere Daniel Deveau, C.S.C. of Father Dick's death shortly thereafter, asked if Pere Deveau was surprised:

"and I answered 'no'. There was something radical about Dick's zeal: I think he would not even have thought about the risks in store. ... I certainly share the idea that Dick died for his faith and for the service of people in need. He was a man of prayer and of deep Christian convictions."[53]

Further, Pere Deveau wrote:

"I have known Dick as an even-tempered young man with a shy smile, yet I never doubted that behind that he had guts, a great courage and a lot of determination. Christ's words "Don't be afraid!" had already resounded profoundly in

---

[53] Deveau, Pere Daniel, C.S.C., letter to Mary Ann Novak, dated January 8, 2008

his soul. There was something in him that reminds me of St. Therese of the Child Jesus: simplicity, genuineness and daily quiet determination. When I hear someone mention "that good men die young", I think about [Richard]. I can say that in my younger years as a religious I met a dedicated young religious in whom there was no falsehood and no vain pretense. He truly was a disciple of Christ, and his death simply cannot have been worthless: he had too much price in the eyes of God."[54]

As Father Alfred D'Alonzo, C.S.C., showed in his extensive discussion of martyrdom in his paper on Father William Evans, C.S.C., who was murdered in Bangladesh in 1971, "It is widely understood that a Christian Martyr is one who gives his life for the tenets of his faith, who gives witness to his faith, who dies while performing acts of mercy."[55]

In an undated note in the Holy Cross Eastern Province Archives, Fr. DePrizio wrote to "Father Bob" [presumably McKee] thanking him for a letter regarding Father Novak: "I really think that given his good intentions, etc. we have a martyr for our Missions. I knew him well—through the years—

[54] Deveau, Pere Daniel, C.S.C., letter to Mary Ann Novak, dated May 11, 2008

[55] Dacono, Rev. Alfred F., C.S.C., PhD, "The Story of Fr. William Evans, C.S.C., Missioner and Martyr," pages 7, 33-34

have a great deal of his correspondence and have been amazed at the charity of the man and priest." Tantalizingly, he concludes the short note with: "More later. See you in Rome."

Father Willy Raymond wrote to me:

"I entered the seminary in the fall of '64 so your brother Richard was already considered a martyr in Holy Cross at that time and as a new seminarian I was very interested in the heroism of this young priest who was killed while on a mission of charity."[56]

Three of Father Novak's siblings have visited Bangladesh since his death. His brother James lived and worked there for many years, mostly because of Father Novak, and he wrote a book on the country, as mentioned earlier. He told family members, on his first visit there in the early 1970s, that he received a call from the hotel manager just after he got to his room, who said some people were in the lobby for him. Since he was not expecting anyone, he went down mostly out of curiosity. A long line of Bengali men and women were waiting quietly in a line, and as Jim came out of the elevator, they came toward him and one by one, kissed his hand and told him how much they loved and revered Father

---

[56] Raymond, Rev. Wilfred J, C.S.C., National Director, Family Theater Productions, email to Mary Ann Novak, November 8, 2007

Novak and wanted to pay their respects to his family.

In December 1996, at a memorial service held in Dhaka for Father Novak's brother James Novak, the student nurse whose family Father Novak had sought that final day in 1964 approached Jim's family members to give her condolences on Jim's death, and to assure them that Father Novak's charity would never be forgotten.

Likewise, Father Novak's brother Michael has had several instances reminding him of the young priest's effect: An older worker at the Dacca Hilton in the late 1980s hurried across the lobby to him, took his cuff, and asked if he was the brother of Father Novak? On Michael's nod, the Bangladeshi knelt down and kissed his sleeve, saying it was respect for Father Richard, whom he regarded as a good man, and whose memory he continued to reverence. More recently, in Brussels in about 2000 at a conference on democracy, two Bangladeshis approached Michael at the dinner to tell him that Fr. Richard's memory is still cherished in Dhaka. And within the last few years in Casablanca, a Lebanese Muslim engaged to a Bangladeshi related to Michael that his fiancée spoke to him about Father Richard, of how he was still fondly remembered, and that some said there should be a public statue to him.

Father Novak's nephew Joseph, son of James Novak, is currently serving as Political officer in the U.S. Embassy in Indonesia and recently received a note from a former U.S. Ambassador to Bangladesh:

"It is great to hear from you. While I never knew your father, I did read about and learn much about your uncle from long-serving priests teaching at Notre Dame, the Archbishop and freedom fighters. Father Richard is admired to this day."[57]

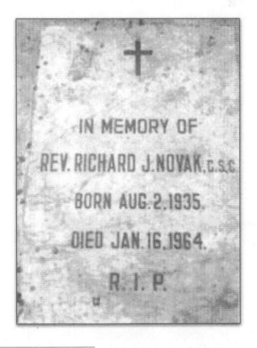

[57] Thomas, Harry K., Jr., former U.S. Ambassador to Bangladesh, now Director General of the Foreign Service, in an email to Joseph L. Novak, May 20, 2008

There are many more stories his family has related of people contacting them around the world. In about 1967, Michael received a clipping which said that "a horse named Father Richard finished in first place in Calcutta in the seventh race." Another story is of special interest: Michael Novak and his wife Karen were planning to travel to Dhaka for the dedication of the Father Richard Novak Memorial Library at Notre Dame College in August of 1995. When Michael went to the Bangladeshi embassy in Washington to pick up their visas, he was asked to wait until the Ambassador arrived. An hour passed, and he began to think their visas were being denied. Another half hour later, the Ambassador explained that he had wanted to personally thank Michael as the brother of Father Novak to whom the Ambassador felt he owed his career. Father Novak had been his logic teacher at Notre Dame College and in that year of schooling, he himself had won the national prize in logic, which he credited to "Father Novak being such an extraordinary teacher." That award greatly advanced his reputation and career, he said, and that is what led to him becoming Ambassador to the United States of America.

I had the pleasure of meeting that same Ambassador at a reception at the new Bangladeshi embassy in Washington, and directly heard his words of gratitude for Father Novak. Several other diplomats who had also studied under him remembered him with reverence. I was constantly reminded by people during my visit to Bangladesh in 1983 how much effect Father Novak had had on so many in his short 15 months there. Many still remembered him, and prayed for him and to him. I was introduced everywhere I went as the sister of Father Novak, and the reactions of Bangladeshis were very moving those 20 years after his death.

Pope John Paul II told Michael that he had remembered Father Novak at the Mass he celebrated during his 1986 visit in Dhaka. In 2003, at Santa Maria in Trastevere in Rome, Michael Novak came by surprise upon a ceremony honoring the martyrs of religious orders of the 20th century. One by one, names were read aloud of those members of religious orders who had been killed, and a candle was lit for each one. The name of Father Richard J. Novak, C.S.C., along with that of Father William Evans, C.S.C., was read aloud, and two candles were lit in the darkness.

VI.
Conclusion

I hope this short book recalls this young priest to Holy Cross, and clears away some of the misconceptions and mysteries surrounding his character, his life and his death, even as I continue to explore unresolved issues. In 1964, only a few, sparse details of Father Novak's death were revealed to the Novak family. Somehow, perhaps inadvertently, the family was left with the impression that Father Novak had acted imprudently. Over the years, the family has learned that a few of his colleagues in Bangladesh were angry at him. Some gave the impression that he had gone out that day on his own, unbidden, reckless, independent and immature. One suggested that he was disobeying orders. It is possible that Dick's characteristic courage, independence, and religious zeal, prized by some of his Superiors, did not always sit so well with others in Dacca. For the family's part, parents and siblings were willing to wait for the judgment of the Church and of history, and we really did not know enough about the details.

When I began searching the archives in earnest in 2006-07, I discovered that others knew important details soon after his death and that these details were meticulously committed to writing. Maybe others in the community thought that they knew more than they did; certainly there is evidence in the records that they wanted to spare Richard's mother Irene, in particular, many of the gruesome details.

In any case, witnesses and records now put to rest two major concerns raised about Father Richard's actions on January 16, 1964. There is conclusive evidence that Father Novak was asked to go by Sister Lourdes to undertake a mission of mercy and that he did not go out on his own during the riots. Second, there is conclusive evidence that Father Richard sought out and received permission to go out to see what he could find regarding the Hindu family of the nurse in the hospital—a nurse he had never met. As the Principal of Notre Dame College, Father Bill Graham, put it in his remarks on Father Novak's disappearance and death:

> "For Father Novak it did not matter that he had never seen the family, had never seen the employee concerned. Here was a good deed to

be performed, an opportunity to put into action his desire to be of service. And for him a task undertaken had to be completed. ... He never reached his destination. Yet, in a more profound sense, he gloriously arrived at his goal: He gave his life in a journey of charity."[58]

We do not know the motive for the attack on him. The issue of robbery as a motive is unclear from the records we have. We do not yet know enough about the killers, their previous and later histories, though it was an email received in 2003 referring to one of those killers serving as a 'bat boy' to a jailed journalist friend of James Novak that sharpened my interest in learning more.

We do not know if the death sentence against Yunus Ali, who was seen and convicted of stabbing Father Novak to death, was ever carried out. Nor have we found any records to verify that they were all released in 1972 following the general amnesty after the War of Independence.

We do not know what happened to his personal belongings, his cassock and other clothes, his bicycle, his watch, his holy cross, except to assume that those identified by Father Burke and McKee were taken by the police as evidence for the trial and retained by them. We do have two sets of his

---

[58] "Principal's Message," Memories of Father Richard J. Novak, C.S.C., in Blue and Gold dedicated to him, undated

glasses in the Michael Novak Archives at Stonehill College, though it is not clear which of these he was wearing on January 16, 1964.

Above all, we do not know for sure what happened to his body. The stories related to us are conflicting and confusing. Newspaper articles at the time of this death, and again at the time of the trials of the murderers, spoke of his body having been found. Then, on August 21, 1995 at the consecration of the Novak Library at Notre Dame College in Dhaka, an old man approached Michael Novak and grasped his hand tightly. The man was unusually tall, Michael related to me, and he said he had been the detective at the time of the murder. This detective told Michael he had discovered a detached skull long the river bank, and had taken it to a dentist, and achieved positive identification of Father Novak's teeth. Can this be verified? Who was the dentist? Is that skull in Father Novak's memorial grave in Dacca? I intend to continue seeking the answers to these questions.

The tasks ahead are something like a detective story. Many records are incomplete, missing, or contradictory, such as which church in Dhaka holds or held the altar and tabernacle donated in memory of Anna and Ben Sakmar? Also, many records have yet to be fully searched or obtained, particularly from the National Archives in the United States and in the Bangladeshi courts. Moreover, I have not found nor reached all those who might know of these long-ago events in 1964. I hope to track down these witnesses in the days ahead and more completely document Father Novak's life and death.

Afterword

As I write this, Vatican Information Service provides a news article of Pope Francis meeting with the Superiors General on November 29, 2013 where the Pope discussed the identity and mission of consecrated life:

"A radical approach is required of all Christians, the Pope stated, but religious persons are called upon to follow the Lord in a special way: 'They are men and woman who can awaken the world. Consecrated life is prophecy. God asks us to fly the nest and to be sent to the frontiers of the world, avoiding the temptation to 'domesticate' them. This is the most concrete way of imitating the Lord." The Pope also announced that 2015 will be dedicated to consecrated life, the year following the 50th Anniversary of Father Novak's death, and it is my hope that the many religious martyrs will again be recognized by the Church.

I first thought I had a chance to learn more directly from the trial documents when I received a note from a friend to Holy Cross, Professor Lawrence Gomes from the University of Wisconsin, who introduced himself to me in an email: "Your last name really caught my attention. In my first year at Notre Dame College in Dhaka after high school matriculation, my logic professor was Fr. Novak; I still distinctly remember him, so young and vibrant, yet so placid in nature." He then offered his assistance in learning more about Father Novak's death during his return trips to Bangladesh to visit his Mother, and he was able to confirm that the court papers/transcripts related to the trials in 1964 and 1966 are part of Bangladesh court records, though with no computerized documentation back then, the papers may be impossible to locate or indeed may be turned to dust by now. While I have not found a way to instigate a search for the documents, the weapon used, his clothes or other belongings held by the Courts in Dhaka, it has been good to ascertain they are there and not turned over to Pakistan after independence was declared in 1971.

Early in 2013, Michael got a letter from a priest in Canada, Fr. Art Seaman, who had spent the summer of 1958 with Richard at St. Joseph's Oratory in Montreal, along with Fr. Bill Condon. They became friends, traveled to Quebec City together and kept in touch via Christmas letters until Richard's letters stopped coming. Fr. Seaman writes: "I figured he was too busy to carry on the correspondence until, one day, I read a brief item in a Catholic paper that the murderers of Fr. Richard had been tried and convicted. Hence, he has been one of my un-canonized saints for these many years. ... I'm telling the story often about making contact with the brother and sister of my private 'Saint Richard.'"

Another note I received was from a Holy Cross priest who had roomed near him at the Foreign Mission Seminary in 1962: "I have nothing to add to your research, but I wanted you to know that your work has been appreciated by one who knew Dick before he went to Bangladesh. Indeed, I 'inherited' one of the shirts he left behind, which I wore until it succumbed to age. I'm sorry now that I didn't keep it as a relic."

Many Holy Cross priests and brothers have written me notes, glad that Father Dick is being remembered. While this paper was mostly written as an exploration of the death of my brother, I soon learned that it was an also an examination of his short life. One moment on that ferry across the Lakya River, on that muddy bank, had eclipsed everything he was and had done in his 28 years of life, and suppressed my memories of him. Looking at him that way, his death has given him eternal life, a priest forever in the order of Melchizedek.

Appendix:
Funeral Eulogy

"Unless the grain of wheat falling into the ground die, itself remains alone. But if it die, it brings forth much fruit," John 12:24.

Your Excellency, Right Reverend and Very Reverend Monsignori, Brother Priests, dear Sisters, Parents, Members of the Family, Relatives and Friends of Father Richard Novak.

The life of every human being has a special meaning. As every human personality is unique, so does every human life have its special expression and purpose—distinct, different from all others.

If in the physical order the God of Creation can see to it that no two faces, no two sets of fingerprints, no two types of handwriting are identical, with what even greater endless variety are marked the lines of beauty, action and design of each individual human soul.

Here is part of the measure of the greatness of each human being: not only that he is made to the image and likeness of God, but that he writes a script and walks a path all his own, and in so doing gives his personal measure of glory to God.

It is perhaps good for us to recall and to meditate this truth now. For as we gather here to pray for Father Richard Novak, we might be tempted to think: "What an untimely death."

But no! We cannot say this at all. There is no such thing really as an untimely death. A lifetime is lived—and it is lived in its completeness in a few years, or in a single breath, or in the first and only throb of human life, just as well as a lifetime is lived in a hundred years of activity. And each of these lives, short or long, gives its own measure of glory to God.

What is the meaning of a man's life? It is as simple and as profound as this. If he lives, he lives a lifetime; complete, unique in its meaning and glory.

At a time like this, under these heartbreaking circumstances, it is best that we seek for this special significance in the life of him whom we mourn. At such a time oratory would be inappropriate; an appeal to the emotions would be too cruel for us to bear.

Surely the thought of the meaning of the life of Father Novak has been much in your minds as it has been in mine. To each of us it will have its personal implications. I can only tell you what it means to me.

For the past few days one quotation has been running through my mind—Our Lord's words: "If the grain of wheat ... falling into the ground ... die, it brings forth much fruit."

And though the illustration used here is simple to understand when related to the realm of plant life, when applied as the Master Sower Christ does here to human life, it contains a great mystery. It is a mystery akin to and intimately connected with the mystery of Christ's own death and Resurrection.

Richard Novak was a young boy and, I understand from talking with his family, an active eager boy.

He was a young man and, again I understand, an alert intelligently curious young man.

He was a religious of the Congregation of Holy Cross, and he was a sincere religious.

He was a priest of God, and he was a zealous priest.

It was as a religious and as a priest that I knew him. But, above all, I knew him as a missionary, and to this I can add no more than that he was a self-sacrificing one.

He was interested in so many different things; he wanted to try so many endeavors—and there is something attractive about a questing spirit.

He was one of the most fearless young men I ever met—and there is something gallant and even awesome in such fearlessness.

And he was one of the most selfless young men I ever knew—and there is a beauty and wonder all its own in complete selflessness.

In his earlier life he sometimes gave the impression of not quite reaching a final decision, of never being quite satisfied with his goals in life. It was only when he discovered something worthy of his effort and personality that he really found himself. His questing spirit, his fearlessness, his selflessness—which gave him an almost perfect innate mission adaptability, a rare gift—these qualities finally met their match in the challenge of the missionary vocation he chose.

We had many talks together, Father Richard and I, at the Foreign Mission Seminary in Washington.

And it began to be apparent to me that here was a young man not of the regular mold, but one looking for an outstanding challenge.

He found it in the decision, approved by Superiors, to dedicate his life to the apostolate to the Moslems, admittedly one of the most difficult of all apostolates. In twelve hundred years Christianity has never really built a bridge to Islam. Yet, this is what Father Richard chose, and went off questing fearlessly and selflessly to Pakistan, where his Holy Cross confreres work in this largest Moslem country in the world.

That was not quite a year and a half ago. He first studied the language and customs of the country, then enrolled for advanced studies at the University of Dacca. He was studying Arabic and Islamics, the work was started, the promise of the future career was bright. And then the Finger of God reached down, and it was all over.

There is a sort of perfect unity in Father Richard's life in that, as far as we know, he met death, like Christ, in the midst of the people he had come to help and succor. And from what we know he also met death on an errand of mercy, trying to help those who were threatened by the communal Hindu-Moslem riots that were raging in and around Dacca.

If it be said that it would have been more prudent to have stayed under cover at such a time, let us again remember that Father Novak was completely fearless and selfless, and so all that really mattered is that there was a mission of mercy to be performed.

We might recall that the very next words of Our Lord in St. John's Gospel following the illustration of the grain of wheat are: "He that loveth his life shall lose it; and he that hateth his life in this world keepeth it to life everlasting." Father Novak did not value his life above his concern for others. Would to God that each of us dies so well pointed on charity's target!

The official designation of "martyr" by the Church is a special one subject to many conditions. But in the fuller, deeper sense of the word, "a martyr is one who dies giving witness to Christ."

In this full, deep sense Father Richard Novak died a martyr. He had chosen a life in a mission field where perhaps the greatest work the mission-ary can do is just to be present and bear witness to Christ. Conversions? Almost non-existent. The best one can do at times is to live and suffer, and study and pray, and die an inch at a time.

But the usual way is not enough for unusual souls. And so the grain of wheat, the seed, fell to the ground and died in an instant.

The sacrifice, the total sacrifice of life, has been made. We know now what it is. Certainly Father Richard's parents and brothers and sister know what sacrifice really is. So, too, Father's religious province, which has lost two young men of unusual ability in Pakistan in less than four years, knows what missionary sacrifice is. And so do his confreres in Pakistan who have seen this young man die in the good cause.

Yes, we know the sacrifice made. But we may never know the full consequences of this sacrifice. The grain of wheat has died and will now bring forth much fruit. The Sower, Christ, has promised it.

All we can safely say today is that in the mission fields of Pakistan and through the Church there has been let loose a new and most precious flood of God's grace, evoked by the death of this latest missionary martyr.

We can also confidently expect that there will come now new priestly and religious vocations here at home in the diocese where he lived, and new missionary vocations to take his place overseas.

Finally, all of us will go through the rest of our lives knowing that our experience has been enriched by the meaning of this man's life and death, and by the unique glory that his life and death gave to God.

One brief word at the end. To his parents—good mother, good father—the heartfelt sympathy of each one of us here, and of all the others who are with us here in spirit.

There is a grief of hopelessness leading to bitter frustration. And there is a grief of faith which ennobles. We know that yours is this grief of faith and that each tear is a prayer that says to God, "I believe. Thy Will be done."

Yours is a faith that knows better than any of us here that if your Richard has given his life and body to be planted in the furrow of the earth like a seed, that it is only that he might blossom to new beauty, to a completely happy resurrection, to a never-ending Heaven with Jesus and Mary.

May he rest in peace. Amen.

Rev. Arnold A. Fell, C.S.C.
Johnstown, Pennsylvania
January 27, 1964

About the Author

Mary Ann Novak has been working on energy and power matters in the public and private sectors for over 30 years, including several years on Wall Street. As an independent consultant, Ms. Novak provides select private sector clientele with strategic planning, research, and issue analysis, document assistance, oral coaching, business development support, and personal government representation.

She has extensive experience with Congress, the Executive Branch, and with the global energy industry. Ms. Novak has served as Principal Deputy and Acting Assistant Secretary of Nuclear Energy in the U.S. Department of Energy, as well as a Vice President of Parsons Brinckerhoff, a global engineering firm. Over her active career, Ms. Novak has represented the Governor of Michigan in Washington, and served as Counselor to a Deputy Secretary of Energy, as well as an executive assistant to the President and CEO of David McKay Publishers, Inc.

She is a member of the John Carroll Society, the Downtown Washington SERRA Club, and the Nevada Test Site Historical Association. Ms. Novak is an avid reader and traveler, primarily visiting countries in Europe and Asia. She is studying to be a lay Dominican with the Immaculate Conception Chapter at the Dominican House of Studies.

Made in the USA
San Bernardino, CA
07 February 2014